Christmas Through Our Eyes

Three Plays For Youth

Rebecca Bergey
and
Rebecca Hunsberger

CSS Publishing Company, Inc., Lima, Ohio

CHRISTMAS THROUGH OUR EYES

Copyright © 1999 by
CSS Publishing Company, Inc.
Lima, Ohio

The original purchaser may photocopy material in this publication for use as it was intended (i.e. worship material for worship use; educational material for classroom use; dramatic material for staging or production). No additional permission is required from the publisher for such copying by the original purchaser only. Inquiries should be addressed to: Permissions, CSS Publishing Company, Inc., P.O. Box 4503, Lima, Ohio 45802-4503.

ISBN 0-7880-1516-8 PRINTED IN U.S.A.

We would like to thank the following people and dedicate this book to them for their help in creating and/or participating in these plays:
  Daniel Tanner
  Patrick Tanner
  Jason Reifsnyder
  Daniel Bergey
  Rebecca Hunsberger
  Rebecca Bergey
  Matthew McCoy
  Rachel Hunsberger
  Anson Kring
  St. John Center Lutheran Church Senior Choir

We would also like to thank CSS Publishing and Zondervan Publishing for their help in publishing our plays.

A special thank-you goes to our Sunday School teacher, Deb Lorah, who has been our inspiration, motivation, and gift from God. It was her faith in God and her faith in us that reminded us of the importance of putting together our plays. We think this is one of those time when it is not hard to figure out **Where God Is In All This.**

Becca and Becky

Table Of Contents

Three Foolish Men   7

A Home For Christmas   13

A Little Child Shall Lead Them   21

Three Foolish Men

Background and Suggestions

The three young men who comprised the Senior High Sunday School class of St. John Center Lutheran Church in East Earl, Pennsylvania, wrote this play in 1990. It is the story of a diligent search for the baby Jesus by three foolish men. The class performed this play as the closing act of our annual children's Christmas program.

This play can be as simple or as elaborate as you need or want. Movement of characters will depend upon the setting in which this play is presented. This play is written to include a reference to East Earl, the name of the town where it was originally performed. East Earl is in the middle of the Pennsylvania Dutch country; therefore, the smells of farmers fertilizing their fields are common. If possible, substitute a name of a local town which begins with East.

While the play was not written to accompany a project or challenge, the current Sunday School class has determined that a mission project could easily complement it. The closing play dialogue reminds us that we do not need a star to guide us to see Jesus. He can be seen in everyone around us. Any of the following projects, or similar challenges, will help to focus both play participants and their audience on the fact that we can see the face of Jesus daily by looking to others:
- Collect and deliver small gifts needed by local nursing home residents
- Determine if there are items needed by local homeless shelters or halfway houses
- Help a charity or mission project of your choice

Three Foolish Men

Cast of Characters:
Narrator
Daniel — Foolish man
Jeremiah — Foolish man
Joshua — Foolish man

Scene I:
In Brooklyn.

Scene II:
At the airport.

Scene III:
In East Earl.

Scene IV:
In any church sanctuary.

Scene I

Narrator: This is the story of three foolish men. They, too, saw the great star in the heavens on that first Christmas Eve. Their intent was much the same as the three wise men — to follow the star and find the long-awaited Messiah, the baby Jesus. However, as you will soon see, these three foolish men have had their share of trouble in following the right star.

(All three men enter stage looking confused.)

Joshua: Where are we going?

Jeremiah: We were following the star but now it's gone.

Joshua: So where are we?

Daniel: *(Using calculator)* By my calculations, we took a wrong turn at that last traffic light. That should mean we are in Brooklyn.

Joshua: Brooklyn?

Jeremiah: Look, it's a star! Let's follow it! It's moving real fast. We'd better hurry.

Joshua: I remember a time when you said this trip would only take a couple of days. One thousand nine hundred and ninety years *(change year according to the year performed)* later we're still looking for this baby. He's probably grown up by now. We won't recognize him when we do find him. I'm tired and I don't like this place called Brooklyn. There are people here with green and orange hair and it smells really bad. I say we follow this star and find this baby.

Jeremiah: That star is getting smaller and smaller *(measures the sky with ruler)*, and if we don't leave now we will never find this baby.

(All exit stage.)

Scene II

Narrator: And so our three foolish men were on their way once again, following the wrong star, still looking for the baby Jesus. This time their journey takes them to the airport.

(All three enter stage still looking confused.)

Jeremiah: I don't see that star anywhere. It looked like this was the place where it came to a stop.

Joshua: Wait ... over there! That's our star! Let's go!

(All run across stage but do not exit.)

Jeremiah: *(Bewildered)* It took off without us. Now what will we do?

Joshua: I remember a time when you said the star would come to rest over the place where the baby was.

Daniel: Obviously, we have been chasing a plane and not the star. Be calm. We've been in this situation before. I suggest we ask those fine people over there for their advice. They are at least dressed similar to us ... maybe they too are searching for the baby.

Joshua: *(Muttering, shaking head)* I remember a time when no one with self-respect would have shaved his head and sold flowers. This place called Brooklyn sure is strange.

(All exit stage.)

Scene III

Narrator: And so our friends continue on their journey, always searching, ever hopeful of finding the baby Jesus.

(All enter stage with map.)

Daniel: I certainly hope those people knew what they were talking about when they told us to go east. By the way, where are the camels?

Jeremiah: It's not my fault. No one ever told me camels couldn't swim across the river.

Daniel: You *do* still have the gold, frankincense, and myrrh? You didn't give it to those beggars, did you?

Jeremiah: No, of course not! It's all safe on the camels. *(Pauses)* Too bad the camels didn't make it across the river.

Joshua: So where are we now?

Daniel: *(Consulting map)* We are in the fields of East Earl.

Joshua: Well, can we move on? This place doesn't smell any better than Brooklyn!

Jeremiah: Look at that big building. There's a strange glow coming from its windows. That has to be the star. Come on!

(All exit stage.)

Scene IV

Narrator: Will this be another wild goose chase? Have our three foolish men followed the wrong star one more time? Will they ever find this baby Jesus for whom they have so diligently and faithfully searched? Before we just quickly laugh at these men we should pause to consider what sort of world this would be if we all were more faithful and diligent in our search for Jesus. What directions would our lives take if we too believed the word of God with such intensity and such enthusiasm that we would spend years searching for the promised baby?

(All enter stage.)

Daniel: *(Daniel and Joshua are walking around center aisle, looking around in amazement)* What is this place?

Joshua: I don't know, but at least this place is better than Brooklyn. These people have *hair* and it's not strange colors.

Jeremiah: *(If possible, shouts from balcony)* There's no baby in swaddling clothes up here. *(Comes down to join others, but never gives up looking for the baby)*

Daniel: It's obvious that the baby isn't here. Maybe we should have tried *East* Los Angeles instead of *East* Earl.

Joshua: You're right, the baby is not here. Let's go find another star. One of these days we are going to find that baby Jesus, I just know it.

Jeremiah: *(Still looking at congregation carefully, walking up and down aisles)* Wait! Just wait a minute ... Look at these faces ... Look carefully. *(Others look at congregation carefully, walking up and down aisles)* Can you see? ... We have found Jesus! He is here! *(Excitedly)* You can see him in every one of these faces ... Jesus is within each and every person here ... When one person looks at the other he sees Jesus!

Daniel and Joshua: You are right. Jesus is here!

All Three: Alleluia!

A Home For Christmas

Background and Suggestions

Two young women and two young men wrote this play. Their goal was to write a play about being homeless at Christmas. Gradually, the similarities between the real Christmas story and what we were trying to write became clear.

The Senior High Sunday School class performed this play as the first and final act for our annual children's Christmas program. The play is written so that any children's program may be inserted in the middle, whether that is recitations or another play.

This play can be as simple or as elaborate as you need or want it to be. Movement of characters will depend upon the setting in which this play is presented. In our experience, a bicycle helmet made the perfect prop for an expectant mother.

It became apparent that a class could not write a play that challenges action from the audience without taking that same challenge to heart. The class contacted a local shelter for abused women to determine its needs. We responded with a toy collection project for the children in this shelter. Toys were wrapped and delivered by the youth before Christmas.

A Home For Christmas

Cast of Characters:

    Mary — pregnant woman
    Joe — Mary's husband
    Ms. Jergusen — church member
    Mr. Andersen — church member
    Shelter Personnel — non-speaking role(s)
    Choir

Scene I:
    Sanctuary of any church.

Scene II:
    Homeless shelter.

Scene III:
    Sanctuary of any church.

Scene I

(The choir begins the program by leading the congregation in singing "Joy To The World." Choir and congregation sing first verse only. As the organist begins second verse with an introduction, Mary and Joe make their entrance down the center aisle. Mary is pregnant and both are poorly dressed. The couple appears to be looking for a seat. They speak quietly with several "planted" people who have been instructed to refuse their request for a seat. The music suddenly quits as the couple nears the front of the sanctuary. Ms. Jergusen rises from the congregation and walks to the front of the sanctuary to confront the couple.)

Ms. J: Excuse me. May I help you?

Joe: We heard the music and thought we could stay for the service. Besides, we have nowhere else to go.

Ms. J: We don't have room for people like you. Please leave. There is a homeless shelter down the street that will be able to help you. If you turn right when you leave the church you will have no problem finding the shelter.

(Mary and Joe turn and exit the sanctuary by the rear door. As Ms. Jergusen returns to her seat, Mr. Andersen stands to talk with her. If possible, Mary and Joe prepare to enter the front of the sanctuary from an entrance near the front.)

Mr. A: Why did you just kick out those homeless people?

Ms. J: Well, I didn't think the congregation would want that kind of people here.

Mr. A: This is a church. God accepts everyone into his house.

Ms. J: Yeah, I know. But they don't belong in this church. Did you see the way they were dressed?

Mr. A: Yes, but does their faith in God have anything to do with the way they dress?

Ms. J: Oh, I see what you mean. Maybe I should do something to make it up to them. I'll take some canned food over to the shelter.

Mr. A: You can take the food, but I don't think that's what you should be doing.

(Mr. Andersen returns to his seat. Ms. Jergusen leaves the sanctuary by the back door and prepares for her entrance in the front of the sanctuary.)

Scene II

(Mary and Joe enter the sanctuary through the front doors. Mary is walking wearily.)

Mary: Dear, I think that we are lost.

Joe: What are you talking about? We're not lost!

Mary: I'm tired. Why don't we stop and ask for directions?

Joe: No, I know where we are going. Let's just keep walking.

Mary: But, Joe, my feet are swollen. I just can't walk anymore. *(Pauses. Looks to ceiling and continues to speak in awe)* Look at that star! Remember the star in your dream that you described to me? Do you want to follow it to see where it will lead us?

Joe: You're right! It is the star in my dream. This star will lead us to a safe place. Let's go. I'll help you. I know we can make it to the shelter.

(They exit by another door in the front of the sanctuary. As they leave, a sign that says "Homeless Shelter" is displayed. Other props include a small table and chairs. Mary and Joe enter by a door near the altar. They are greeted by Shelter Personnel who show them to a table.)

Joe: This is a really nice place. I'm glad we were able to find it.

Mary: I agree. It does feel good to have a warm place to rest for a while. It almost feels like home.

(Ms. J enters by the same door. She is carrying a small bag of food. She approaches Mary and Joe.)

Ms. J: Hello again. Look, I felt bad about what I said to you back at church. I thought I would make up for that by giving you this bag of food.

Joe: *(Sarcastically)* Gee, thanks.

Mary: It's not that we don't appreciate your gift of food, but sometimes you have to give of yourself as well.

Ms. J: I guess there's nothing I can do to make up for the way I acted. And you are right. Sometimes giving money or food isn't always what's needed. Sometimes we have to give of ourselves. *(Pauses to think for a moment)* We're having a children's Christmas program back at church. Why don't you come back with me and enjoy the program? We'll be singing some Christmas carols and you'll be able to hear the Christmas story. Please say you'll come with me.

(Mary and Joe look at each other and nod in affirmation.)

Joe: Maybe we should go. It might be where the star was supposed to lead us.

(All three leave by the same door they entered. Choir and congregation will sing the second verse of "Joy To The World." All characters return to sanctuary by back doors and seat themselves in the front of the sanctuary for the children's program.)

Insert any children's program here

Scene III

(The children's program ends with the singing of verses 3 and 4 of the hymn "Joy To The World." After the children's program, the play continues as the four characters stand for the following dialogue.)

Mary: This has been a wonderful evening. Thank you for inviting us back to see the play. That was really nice of you.

Ms. J: I'm sorry I was so rude to you before.

Joe: That's okay. We're just glad that you invited us back to see the play. It was a wonderful gift just to see the little children. Someday maybe our own child will be in a Christmas play.

Mr. A: It's been a pleasure having you here. I think this will be a Christmas that we will all long remember.

(These four characters all turn so that they face away from the congregation. They alter their appearance in some manner: Joe removes his hat, Mary removes her shawl, Ms. J pulls her hair back, Mr. A takes off his jacket. All four turn around to face the congregation again.)

Joe: Our hope for this Christmas is that we will remember that God's greatest gift to us was his son, Jesus.

Ms J: We also hope that all of us will remember that Christmas doesn't mean buying gifts.

Mary: It means that we give ourselves to those who need us the most.

Mr. A: There is joy in giving what can't be bought — love.

(Choir will sing hymn "Holy Child Within The Manger" [found in With One Voice, *hymn #638] or another hymn which speaks of Jesus' birth and ministry to those who are strangers and outcasts.)*

(Original play ended with this dialogue. Adjustments to be made for each individual circumstance.)

Mary: Our Sunday School class will be delivering toys to the children living at the Clare House in Lancaster this week. The Clare House is a place where homeless people can go for help with their lives. We'd like to challenge everyone here tonight to do something for someone who does not have a home for Christmas.

A Little Child Shall Lead Them

Acknowledgment

We gratefully acknowledge the use of a "Christmas Carol to Shop By." Taken from *Holiday Ideas for Youth Groups* by Wayne Rice and Mike Yaconelli. Copyright © 1981 by Youth Specialties, Inc. Used by permission of Zondervan Publishing House.

Background and Suggestions

Two young women and two young men wrote this play. They acted out their dreams of the future by choosing their fantasy occupations and lives. A younger child was asked to help with the play.

The Senior High Sunday School class performed this play as the closing act for our annual children's Christmas program. This play can be as simple or as elaborate as you need or want it to be. Movement of characters will depend upon the setting in which this play is presented.

As this play developed, the idea to give everyone in the audience a Christmas card evolved. A simple star was chosen as a logo of sorts. This star also graced the front of our play programs. To make the cards, we used blue construction paper and glued a white star on the front. The words "A Little Child Shall Lead Them" were printed in crayon on the inside.

The hymn, "Infant Holy, Infant Lowly," was taken from *Lutheran Book of Worship,* hymn #44.

A Little Child Shall Lead Them

Cast of Characters:
    Numbers — an accountant
    John — a newly elected U.S. Senator
    Ruth — a marine biologist
    Anna Maria — a Spanish professor
    Bob — a kid from the neighborhood
    Narrator
    Choir

Scene I:
    At campaign headquarters after John has won the Senatorial election. Action moves to John's home as John and his good friends gather for an evening together.

Scene II:
    At Ruth's townhouse.

Scene III:
    At the shopping mall with John and Numbers.

Scene IV:
    At John's home on Christmas Eve.

Scene I

(Action takes place at campaign headquarters after John has won the Senatorial election. Streamers, balloons, and political posters may be used to decorate. Lights are dimmed. Narrator takes position at microphone. John takes position at a podium as his speech will be made to the audience. Lights are turned on.)

Narrator: Our story begins at the campaign headquarters of John McCoy. He's just won the Senate race in his state by a landslide margin and is enjoying the celebration with his good friends, Numbers, Anna Maria, and Ruth.

John: I just want to thank all those who went out and voted for me. I intend to do my best representing our state in Washington.

Numbers: Congratulations! I know you'll be the best Senator this state has ever had!

Ruth: Great job, John!

Anna Maria: Fantastic! I'm so proud of you!

John: Thanks, guys! I don't know how I could have ever won this election without your support. How can I ever repay you for all that you've done for me?

Ruth: Why not just invite us to your place so that we can have our own little celebration.

John: Good idea ... let's go ...

(Characters leave stage. A change of scenery may be made to show John's living room with a Christmas tree near a window. Action continues with all seated in front of Christmas tree.)

John: You're right, Ruth, it's good to come home and relax with friends. Say, Numbers, did you really think we'd win by such a landslide?

Anna Maria: Now, before you two start reliving the election, Ruth and I think this would be a good time to exchange names for Christmas.

John: Good idea! I'll get some paper.

(John gets paper, pen, and basket from props. John writes names on papers and puts them in a basket. Everyone picks names.)

Anna Maria: *(Looking at name)* Oh, great! I know the perfect gift!

Ruth: Anna Maria, let's go to the kitchen and get some food.

(Ruth and Anna Maria move slowly across stage toward an area set up to resemble a kitchen.)

Ruth: Whose name did you get?

(Anna Maria whispers a name in Ruth's ear. Ruth giggles and their conversation continues quietly as they walk to the kitchen. Once there, they continue to talk quietly and move about the area as if they are preparing food. As the women enter the kitchen area, the conversation turns back to the men.)

Numbers: Who did you get?

John: I got Ruth. Wonder what I should get her? I want to get something really nice for her. Who did you get?

Numbers: I got Anna Maria. I guess I should get something really nice, too. How much were you thinking about spending?

John: I was thinking I could get her this sweater she liked at the mall. It's in the forty dollar range. Have any ideas what you will buy?

Numbers: Well, if you have Ruth and I have Anna Maria, that means they have our names. You can bet that they'll get us something more expensive than a forty dollar sweater. Maybe I could get Anna Maria this leather briefcase that I saw on sale for 75 dollars.

(Ruth opens door from kitchen area acting as though she is throwing a bag of trash outside. She finds Bob on the doorstep. She brings the child into the kitchen area. Both women have puzzled looks on their faces. The women take Bob across the stage toward the men, timing their arrival with the following speech.)

John: Well, maybe I should get something better for Ruth. She was a big help to me during the campaign. She really would like a new stereo. Maybe I should just get that.

Numbers: Here they come. We can talk about this later.

(Ruth, Anna Maria, and Bob approach the men.)

Ruth: John, do you know this kid? We found him sitting on your back deck.

Bob: You're John! Oh, you're the one that's getting the golf clubs ...

Anna Maria: Shhhh! *(Puts hand over Bob's mouth)* How did you hear that?

Bob: My pet snake got loose and I thought it went under your porch. I guess I was listening at the door.

John: Oh, I know who he is. Numbers and I will take him home.

(John, Numbers, and Bob exit by side aisle to back of audience. They continue to talk with Bob as they go. Ruth and Anna Maria find seats by the Christmas tree and begin to snack on the food.)

John: So, Bob, you heard what they're getting us for Christmas? Why don't you tell us? At least tell us how much they are spending!

Bob: Well, it doesn't really matter how much a gift costs. It's the ...

Numbers: It *does* matter how much the gift costs. We have to make sure we get an expensive enough gift.

Bob: Well, actually, a good gift could be one that doesn't cost much.

Numbers: What are you talking about? The best gift is an expensive gift.

Bob: Don't you know that a good gift is one that comes from the heart?

John: I've heard enough out of you. I think we can pick out a good gift ourselves. We won't need any help from a little kid like you.

Numbers: Yeah, let's just take him home so we don't have to listen to him anymore.

(Numbers, John, and Bob exit to rear. Action returns to Ruth and Anna Maria. If possible, Bob returns to back of stage without being seen.)

Anna Maria: Now John heard what I was going to get him. I'll have to get him something different.

Ruth: Yeah, and now they'll be getting something even more expensive than golf clubs so we have to get something even more expensive to top their gifts.

(Numbers and John return to stage by the same aisle they exited. They talk softly with the women as they enjoy an evening of friendship. All talk for a moment or two until the lights are dimmed. Characters move off stage.)

Scene II

(Narrator moves to podium. Ruth and Anna Maria take positions on stage decorated to look like a living room. Lights are turned on.)

Narrator: So it seems our friends have gotten caught up in the commercial side of Christmas. It should be fun to see how this all turns out. Let's join Ruth and Anna Maria as they share a cup of coffee in Ruth's new townhouse.

Anna Maria: This is great coffee. What is it and where did you get it?

Ruth: There's a great new shop in the mall. You'll have to check it out when you go Christmas shopping. And speaking of Christmas shopping, you realize that if I have Numbers' name and you have John's name, that means the guys have our names.

Anna Maria: Yeah, wonder what goofy gift they'll get us. You know how men are when it comes to shopping.

Ruth: Now that's a pretty picture. John and Numbers at the mall!

(Women exit stage as lights are turned off. Men move to center stage. Lights are turned on.)

Scene III

John: I wonder why the mall is so crowded this time of year. This is crazy!

Numbers: Listen, why don't we split up and get our gifts. Let's meet back here in a half hour and then get out of here.

John: Deal. See ya later.

(John and Numbers exit stage by different routes. The following song is sung by the audience. Tune is "Santa Claus Is Coming To Town.")

Song:
    Y'better not mope, Y'better not frown,
    Y'better not keep expenditures down,
    Santa Claus is coming to town.
    Y'better not scrimp, Y'better not save,
    Ya gotta give more than the other guy gave,
    Santa Claus is coming to town.

    So load up all your charge accounts
    And let the payments wait
    And send expensive Christmas cards
    To people you hate, hate, hate!

    Y'better not whine, Y'better not cry,
    Everything's fine just as long as you buy;
    Santa Claus is coming to town.

(Men return to center stage by different doors after the song is finished.)

Numbers: So ... how did it go? What did you get?

John: I'm not finished shopping yet, but here, take a look. *(Opens bag for Numbers to see)*

Numbers: Wow, that's great! Uh, my gift isn't as nice as that. I should go back and get something better. Meet me back here in a half hour.

(Numbers and John exit hurriedly. The same song is sung by the audience a second time.)

Song:
>Y'better not mope, Y'better not frown,
>Y'better not keep expenditures down,
>Santa Claus is coming to town.
>Y'better not scrimp, Y'better not save,
>Ya gotta give more than the other guy gave,
>Santa Claus is coming to town.
>
>So load up all your charge accounts
>And let the payments wait
>And send expensive Christmas cards
>To people you hate, hate, hate!
>
>Y'better not whine, Y'better not cry,
>Everything's fine just as long as you buy;
>Santa Claus is coming to town.

(Numbers and John return to stage at the end of the song. They are carrying shopping bags.)

John: Okay, let's compare gifts again.

Numbers: All right. What do you think of this? *(Opens bag)*

John: Aughh. Now you have a better gift than I do. Ruth will just hate me if her gift isn't as good as Anna Maria's. I'll be right back.

(John exits. Numbers waits around the "mall" until Bob comes ambling by. Bob, with small shopping bag, approaches Numbers from the rear and tugs on his sleeve.)

Bob: Hi. Remember me?

Numbers: Hi ... yeah, I remember you. What are you doing here? This is a big mall. You could get lost.

*(John enters with shirt tail out of pants, sweater pulled off shoulder, hair all mussed up, basically looking very sloppy. He carries a **big** shopping bag of which he is very proud.)*

John: Well, look who it is. I guess he's trying to tell us what the perfect gift is again. Well, Bob, we already have the perfect gift. *(Proudly shows off his new purchase. In a proud voice.)* Take a look at this! *(Opens bag)*

Bob: Well, you know that bigger isn't always better.

John: Well, that's your opinion. Judging by the size of your bag you're not here to buy a big gift. Why are you here?

Bob: I just came for some crayons and paper. I'm going to make my Christmas gifts.

Numbers: Well, this mall is getting more and more crowded. We'll walk you home. *(All begin to exit)* Maybe if you're such an expert on gift buying, you're also an expert on gift wrapping. I don't have a clue how to wrap my gift.

(All exit. Lights are turned off.)

Scene IV

(Narrator moves to podium. All are gathered around the Christmas tree in John's home amid wrapped packages. Lights are turned on.)

Narrator: Well, the plot does thicken, doesn't it? How will this Christmas end? What gifts have these four friends finally decided to give each other? Let's join them on Christmas Eve as they gather once again at John's home.

Anna Maria: Ruth and I can't wait to see what you guys got us. We've had so much fun just thinking of you two at the mall.

Numbers: Let me tell you that the mall is not a fun place at Christmastime. Everyone is pushing and shoving and you had better not want what someone else wants.

John: Yeah, it's a zoo out there. But we managed to get the two biggest and best gifts in the whole mall.

Ruth: Oh, yeah. Well, just wait to see what we got you!

(There's a knock on the door. John answers the door. Bob, holding a card, enters with John.)

John: Look, who's here. Mr. Gift Wizard! Did you come over here to check out our gifts?

Bob: No. I wanted to give you a present that I made special just for all of you. I worked on this a long time. *(Hands a card to John. John reads card to others)*

John: "A little child shall lead them."

Bob: It's my favorite Bible verse, because I'm a little kid and I want to grow up to be just like Jesus. See the star? Wise men follow that star. Well, Merry Christmas!

(Bob exits. Choir members sing hymn "Infant Holy, Infant Lowly." Cast moves to window of John's home and act as if they are listening to carolers. Action continues when choir finishes song.)

Anna Maria: Christmas carolers. It's been years since I've been Christmas caroling. I remember how much fun I had going to people's homes and singing. You know, it was like I was giving them a song as a gift.

Ruth: Did you see Bob's face? He was all excited about his card that he had made. It's been years since I was a little kid making Christmas presents. I'd forgotten how excited I used to get when I made a gift for my parents or my brother. And you know, it didn't really matter what I had made. It seemed that it was more important that I had cared enough to take the time to give something from me.

John: We were so mean to Bob and he still gave us a gift he made with his own hands.

Numbers: Yeah, he didn't spend a lot of time and money at the mall. But his gift reminds me of what Christmas is all about. It's not about buying gifts. It's about giving.

John: It's about the birth of Jesus. Just like the song those carolers were singing.

(Four characters begin to hand out Christmas cards to those in audience.)

Narrator: Our four friends have learned a valuable lesson from a little child. God gave us the gift of his only Son many years ago in a stable in Bethlehem. Let us appreciate his gift to us by giving of ourselves to those around us.

(Narrator waits for cast to return to the stage.)

Narrator: We hope you have enjoyed our gift to you.

(Cast appears on stage for applause and bows.)